Sex and relationships ed

A guide for independent scl..... ...
working with them

Simon Forrest and Simon Blake with Caroline Ray

Department
of Health

SEX
EDUCATION
FORUM

Sex Education Forum

The Sex Education Forum is the national authority on sex and relationships education. The forum was established in 1987 and is based at the National Children's Bureau. It is an umbrella body bringing together over 50 national organisations involved in sex and relationships education. Member organisations work together to share good practice, and to articulate a common voice in support of sex and relationships education for all children and young people.

National Children's Bureau

The National Children's Bureau promotes the interests and well-being of all children and young people across every aspect of their lives. NCB advocates the participation of children and young people in all matters affecting them. NCB challenges disadvantage in childhood.

NCB achieves its mission by
◆ ensuring the views of children and young people are listened to and taken into account at all times
◆ playing an active role in policy development and advocacy
◆ undertaking high quality research and work from an evidence based perspective
◆ promoting multidisciplinary, cross-agency partnerships
◆ identifying, developing and promoting good practice
◆ disseminating information to professionals, policy makers, parents and children and young people.

NCB has adopted and works within the UN Convention on the Rights of the Child.

Published by the National Children's Bureau, Registered Charity number 258825. 8 Wakley Street, London EC1V 7QE. Tel: 020 7843 6000. Website: www.ncb.org.uk

© National Children's Bureau, 2003
Published 2003

ISBN 1 900990 90 3

British Library Cataloguing in Publication Data
A catalogue record for this book is available from the British Library

Contents

Acknowledgements

This booklet is the result of a consultation event held by the Sex Education Forum in March 2002. Thanks are due to all the participants at the event and those people who provided material for or commented on drafts of this resource: Geraldine Wallbank, Kathy Compton, Caroline Davies, Maggie South, Karin O'Sullivan, Sally-Ann Gallivan, Liz Swinden, Julie Lodrick, Richard Gill, Viv Lamb, Emma Gilbert, Siobhan Hawthorne, Moira Rickford, Tony Bennett, Joanne Butcher, Una Archer and Lucy Fogarty. Thank you also to Marilyn Toft, Coordinator, National Healthy School Standard and Sarah Thistle at the Sex Education Forum for their support in facilitating the event and comments on the resource, Gill Frances for comments on the resource and Claire O'Kane for her contribution to Part One. Thank you to Tracey Anderson, Sophie MacGregor and Mark Dunn for administrative support.

Finally, thanks go to Mary Rogers, London Regional Teenage Pregnancy Coordinator for funding the consultation event and the production of this booklet.

Introduction

'I am really pleased you have taken this on – it is so important, I want my children to know about everything.'
Father of an 11 year old

Sex and relationships education (SRE) involves lifelong learning about sex, sexuality, emotions, relationships and sexual health. It supports the acquisition of information, the development of skills and the formation of positive beliefs, values and attitudes to sexual health and well-being. SRE helps children and young people to move with confidence through puberty and adolescence and to manage their lives now and in the future. The Sex Education Forum believes that SRE is an entitlement for all children and young people (Sex Education Forum, 1999a).

'Just because we come from nice homes people think we don't need good sex education and we don't get pregnant.'
Young woman aged 17 years

Children and young people learn about sex and relationships from a wide variety of formal and informal sources, including their family, carers and friends; the media; community and youth work settings; and health services. Although children and young people often say that they want their parents or carers to be their key source of information, recent research has shown that school lessons are the main source of information about sex and relationships for most children and young people (Wellings and others, 2001).

'We found out some stuff from the internet, it was really disgusting – we wanted to ask someone but didn't know who.'
Two boys aged 12 years

Despite the constant pleas from children and young people for school to provide SRE, many schools do not consistently deliver sustained and progressive programmes that are relevant to the maturity and understanding of their pupils. In both the maintained and independent sectors the pressure to achieve academic results, and the lack of support and confidence of teachers in delivery of SRE, contribute to this.

'Many independent schools focus too much on academic
results, but the personal growth side is just as important. Sex
education is a key part of that.'
Teacher, girls school

Sexual health, behaviour and the social policy agenda

The sexual health of young people is a cause for concern in the United Kingdom. The
median age for reported first heterosexual sexual intercourse has fallen to around 17
years old and there has been an increase in the average number of sexual partners
among young people (Wellings and others, 2001). Although more young people report
using condoms at first intercourse, there has also been a steep rise in the number of
young people with STIs. The number of unplanned pregnancies has remained fairly
stable since the 1970s and despite signs of a decrease since 1996, remains the highest
in Europe (Public Health Laboratory Service, 2001; DoH, 2002; UNICEF, 2001).

As well as being at greater risk of adverse health outcomes, young people who become
sexually active before they reach 16 years of age report less satisfaction with their
relationships. Among those young people who have sex before they are 16 years old,
about a third of girls and slightly over a quarter of boys report that it happened too
early. For young women the regret they report is associated with feeling under pressure
to have sex and not planning it with their partner (Wight and others, 2001). The
negative outcome of early and unplanned sex obviously impacts heavily on young
people who are poor or disadvantaged. However the pressures to have sex are
replicated in young people across the class and income spectrum. In reality, all young
people complain that their sex education at home and at school is inadequate, leaving
them ill-equipped for making confident choices regarding their sexual health and well-
being.

The Government is committed to improving the sexual and emotional health of
children and young people through a raft of social policies centred on the Teenage
Pregnancy Strategy (Social Exclusion Unit, 1999), the National Strategy for Sexual
Health and HIV (DoH, 2001) and the National Healthy School Standard (DfEE/DoH
1999). The Teenage Pregnancy Strategy aims to halve the number of conceptions by
under 18 year olds by the year 2010. The National Strategy for Sexual Health and HIV
aims to reduce the number of STIs, including HIV, and identifies young people as a
specific target group.

The National Healthy School Standard (NHSS) is a joint programme, between the
Department for Education and Skills (DfES) and the Department of Health (DoH), that
supports a whole school approach to children and young people's emotional and social
development. The NHSS recognises the need for the whole school environment and
ethos to support and reflect the positive messages about sex and relationships that are

offered within well planned SRE. Schools work towards becoming 'healthy schools' through a local healthy school programme based on the principles and criteria set out within the NHSS. Every Local Education Authority has developed a local programme with their health partners. SRE is one of the eight key themes within the NHSS. Further information on the standard can be found in the document *Guidance and Getting Started – a guide for schools* available from the Wired For Health website (www.wiredforhealth.gov.uk) or by contacting the national team based at the Health Development Agency (see under Key government documents and resources in Appendix 1). A significant number of independent schools are now involved with their local healthy schools programme.

There is recognition that public health targets cannot be met without joined-up action across communities, involving statutory and non-statutory agencies, parents, health professionals and services, and schools. Schools, both independent and maintained, have a clear role to play in ensuring children receive their entitlement to SRE. In 2000, all maintained schools received detailed Government guidance on the organisation, content and delivery of SRE (DfEE, 0116/2000). This resource could prove useful to the independent sector and can be obtained by e-mailing dfes@prologistics.co.uk or phoning 0845 6055560.

SRE in the independent school sector

There is no systematic research available on the quality or quantity of SRE in independent schools. The consultation process that led to the development of this guide confirmed anecdotal evidence that, like the maintained sector, provision is patchy and inconsistent. Furthermore, the consultation suggested the following.

- The emphasis placed on academic standards and achievement in many independent schools means that less attention is paid to providing SRE and other aspects of Personal, Social and Health Education (PSHE) and Citizenship.

- Independent schools are often unwilling to develop SRE because they believe parents and carers will presume there is a problem with high rates of unintended teenage pregnancy in the school, and may consider the school is inappropriate for their child(ren) as a result. Perhaps for the same reason, many local teenage pregnancy coordinators, working to reduce teenage pregnancy through improved sex education and access to contraceptive services, have had difficulties engaging with independent schools.

- Many independent schools provide education for children and young people with a wide range of disabilities and impairments who have particular and specific needs in relation to SRE.

- Many agencies involved in supporting schools do not consider independent schools to be an important target group in terms of SRE, because of their perceived affluence

– even though, in reality the emotional and social development needs of many of these children and young people often go unmet.

■ Many teaching and support staff lack the skills and confidence to deliver SRE.

Participants at the event confirmed that many independent schools are isolated and do not receive support from statutory or voluntary organisations and may be unaware of the training and support that is available to them. All local healthy schools programmes in England have now received national accreditation. The NHSS encourages local programme coordinators to involve all schools in healthy schools activities, including independent schools. Coordinators are currently identifying the most appropriate strategies, within existing resources and government priorities, to encourage this involvement of independent schools.

About this guide

In March 2002, in response to requests for support from local teenage pregnancy coordinators, the London regional teenage pregnancy coordinator commissioned the Sex Education Forum to host a consultation event to identify positive ideas and strategies for developing SRE in schools in the independent sector. The event was co-facilitated with the NHSS. Over 20 colleagues, working within independent schools and in education and health, attended the event and offered ideas, strategies and examples of good practice. These now form the basis of this booklet. This event clarified the following two points.

■ Independent schools should know about and understand the importance of SRE and how to deliver it within the context of PSHE and Citizenship and a whole school approach that promotes emotional health and well-being.

■ Those professionals and organisations who are currently working with schools in the independent sector, and those who are seeking to develop better links with independent schools, need to know more about the independent sector and how it works, and develop more effective shared ways of working.

This guide contributes to meeting these needs. It is divided into Parts 1, 2 and 3.

Part 1 provides an overview of the independent sector.

Part 2 describes how SRE can be delivered in the context of PSHE and Citizenship and identifies additional resources, guidance and sources of support, focusing on schools in the independent sector.

Part 3 is mainly for professionals in education and health working with, or wanting to work with, schools in the independent sector. It offers ideas, strategies and examples of ways in which people have successfully engaged with independent schools.

This guide also contains two appendices.

Appendix 1 lists some useful resources, including the addresses of relevant websites, and information about independent sector organisations and others.

Appendix 2 contains details of publications referred to in the text.

Part 1: **The independent sector**

The Independent Schools Council, a federation of the leading associations in the independent sector, accredits 1,300 schools in the UK. Accreditation is a result of an inspection of a school, which is carried out by a team headed by a former HM Inspector. The school is then subject to further inspection every six years. Results of the inspections are made publicly available on the Council's website (www.iscis.net.uk). This system of inspection does not apply to the 900 schools that are not part of the Independent Schools Council.

The independent sector comprises schools offering both mainstream and special educational provision. Schools range from those providing for fewer than 100 pupils to those accommodating 800 – with the latter being considered a large school (ISIS, 2001). Some schools are specifically for children with special educational needs, such as children and young people with:

- visual and/or auditory impairments
- physical disabilities and impaired mobility
- medical conditions such as epilepsy
- varying degrees of learning disability, including specific learning difficulties such as dyslexia
- autism.

Other independent schools:

- offer provision for gifted children and young people and focus on the highest academic standards
- are experimental and progressive
- have a religious character and cater for children and young people whose parents wish them to be educated in accordance with a specific religious belief. Many of these schools welcome children and young people from different faiths as well as those with no faith
- offer boarding facilities
- are single sex (particularly senior schools)
- offer specialist training in a subject (such as music, dance and drama) alongside the broader academic curriculum.

Independent primary schools fall into two main categories: pre-preparatory, for ages two to seven, and junior or preparatory ('prep') schools, for ages seven to 11 or 13. The title 'preparatory' is used because the last two years are often devoted to preparation for the Common Entrance examination; a pass in which is required for admittance to many independent secondary schools. There are also independent schools for the nursery stages of education; pre-prep departments usually cover the ages two to seven within schools that may go up to ages 11, 12 or 13.

Independent schools receive no grants from public funds and are usually owned and managed under a trust. Some are privately owned and run for profit, while others are charitable foundations. Most have a board of governors that is responsible for the school's finances. The head of the school is normally given freedom to make day-to-day decisions and to choose who to appoint to the staff. There is no requirement for teachers in independent schools to have gained Qualified Teaching Status, although it is increasingly the case that staff in independent schools have achieved this qualification or its equivalent.

Academic standards

Most independent schools offer a similar range of courses to state-maintained schools and enter their pupils for the same public examinations. However, there is often a wider choice of qualifications available, for example some offer the International Baccalaureate. The independent sector is not obliged to teach the National Curriculum and to comply with the associated education targets. Of the 500 schools listed in *The Times* as achieving the highest GCSE results in the year 2000, about 380 were independent schools. More than 80 per cent of pupils at independent schools (including special schools) gain five or more GCSE passes at grade A*–C. This compares with a national average of 45 per cent. Of the independent school A level candidates, 85 per cent gain three or more passes, compared with a national average of 63 per cent. Nine out of ten post-A level leavers from independent schools go on to higher education. At the primary level, most prep schools taking part in the National Curriculum testing report attainment levels well above the national averages (Independent Schools Council website, 2002).

Inspection arrangements

Under the terms of the Education Act 1996, the Secretary of State for Education and Skills appoints a registrar whose duty it is to keep a register of all independent schools in England. This registrar and a team of officials in the DfES also monitor the standards in independent schools to ensure that they meet an acceptable level. The framework for inspection takes into account advice from the Office of Standards in Education (OFSTED), the Independent Schools Inspectorate and local fire authorities on matters relating to school premises, accommodation, instruction and staffing. The inspection framework includes the areas of PSHE and Citizenship. The DfES also seeks advice from local Social Services Inspectorates about standards of care in residential independent schools.

The National Care Standards Commission details criteria for boarding schools. Those schools that provide accommodation to pupils for more than 295 days a year, are likely to be regarded as children's homes and are therefore bound by the National Minimum Standards for children's homes. Those schools that provide boarding for pupils over 16 years of age are subject to the National Minimum Standards for accommodation of pupils under 18 in colleges of further education.

Part 2: **SRE in independent schools**

This section is aimed at those working within independent schools. It describes how SRE can be delivered in the context of PSHE and Citizenship and identifies additional resources, guidance and sources of information and support, as well as giving an overview of approaches and teaching methods.

Ensuring effective sex and relationships education

Research has consistently shown that comprehensive SRE is effective in increasing knowledge among young people, helping them to clarify their attitudes and values and enhancing their emotional and social skills. Effective SRE helps young people delay first sexual intercourse and reduce risk-taking, increases contraceptive use and access to sexual health services (Health Education Authority, 1998; Collins and others, 2002).

The role of PSHE and Citizenship

What is PSHE and Citizenship?
PSHE and Citizenship is the planned provision for the emotional and social development of children and young people. SRE is one aspect of PSHE and Citizenship. PSHE and Citizenship is about helping children and young people to develop a secure sense of identity and to function well in the world. It is the holistic context in which children and young people develop the emotional and social skills that are important if they are to gain the benefit of education about sex, drugs, relationships, alcohol, citizenship, careers, healthy eating, physical activity, safety and active citizenship.

PSHE and Citizenship includes the following three elements:

- the acquisition of accessible, relevant and age-appropriate information
- the development and clarification of attitudes and values that support self-esteem and are positive to health and well-being
- the development of personal and social skills to enable emotional development and interaction with others, as well as the making of positive health choices and active participation in society.

PSHE and Citizenship is provided across the curriculum in all subject areas as well as in planned programmes. The programme in school complements what is learnt at home from parents, carers, family and friends, as well as from wider society.

Why is PSHE and Citizenship important?

It supports the emotional and social development of children and young people. It helps build self-esteem, enables them to participate confidently in lessons and activities, promotes emotional health and well-being and equips them with the knowledge and skills to recognise and manage their feelings as well as to make healthy positive decisions. There is emerging research evidence that positively supporting emotional and social development through PSHE and Citizenship can improve behaviour, attendance and achievement across the curriculum (Rivers and others 1999). PSHE and citizenship is particularly important for children and young people who are living away from home, because they are without the direct day-to-day support of their parents and carers and often rely more heavily on the school for emotional support.

SRE contributes to meeting the aims of the National Curriculum (QCA/DfEE, 1999). Although independent schools are not obliged to work to the National Curriculum they generally work to similar aims, that is:

- to provide opportunities for all pupils to learn and achieve
- to promote pupils' spiritual, moral, social and cultural development and prepare all pupils for the opportunities and responsibilities of adult life.

In meeting these aims, the school curriculum enables pupils to understand their rights and responsibilities; develop enduring values; grow in integrity and autonomy; and develop respect for their environments and their communities. It also promotes pupils' self-esteem and emotional and social development and helps them to form and maintain satisfying relationships. PSHE and Citizenship are central to achieving these aims.

Who teaches PSHE and Citizenship?

In primary and preparatory schools all teachers usually have a large degree of pastoral responsibility for their pupils. In secondary and senior schools, PSHE and Citizenship is usually taught through a tutorial system or by a specialist team of teachers. OFSTED has reported that the most effective PSHE and Citizenship is provided by specialist teams. In both cases the provision should be coordinated by a member of staff who leads the development, monitoring and evaluation of the subject, and who also supports teachers operating in the classroom. This coordinator is most effective when also a member of the senior management team.

In the independent sector, other staff such as the school nurse or housemaster, may have special roles in providing support to small groups or individual pupils, especially in the case of schools with boarders. The roles and responsibilities of the staff should be spelt out clearly in relevant policies. Staff who generally have a less formal relationship may have a particularly valuable role to play. Children and young people often confide in them about their personal worries and concerns, or ask them for information which they are reluctant to ask for in a formal lesson. Staff can provide an effective link to specialist support – within or outside the school – by providing time to talk and paper-based information such as leaflets, and materials obtainable from the public health or health promotion unit within the local Primary Care Trust.

Other professionals from outside the school can support the delivery of SRE and help build links to sources of advice and support in the community. For example, outside speakers add value and interest to a programme taught by teachers, by offering a specialist perspective. They can also provide information about local and national services that children and young people can access – these might include a range of sexual health services and clinics, phone helplines and drop-in centres. All visitors from outside a school who contribute to SRE should be aware of, and work within, the relevant school policies.

The role of the school nurse

(This section is written by Kathy Compton who is a school nurse at Plymouth College)

Where independent schools employ their own school nurse, that nurse is in an ideal position to be involved in the SRE in the school. The roles of independent school nurses vary considerably from a clinical nursing role running a medical centre in a large boarding school, to a public health role within a day school and everything else in between. But all independent school nurses should be involved in SRE in some way.

Individual one to one involvement
Nurses in independent schools are in an ideal position to give one to one confidential advice to pupils about where they can receive contraceptive and sexual health advice and treatment. Confidentiality is a fundamental part of the nurse–pupil relationship and it is a part of her code of conduct. Although a nurse has responsibilities to her employer her duty of confidentiality to their pupils is greater. This relationship is especially useful, as during the PSHE/SRE sessions it is not always appropriate to ask personal questions. Also, due to the differing developmental rates of the pupils, topics are not always addressed appropriately for individual pupils during the classroom sessions. The nurse being available during the school day, and in a boarding situation there may be 24 hour cover, gives the pupils wide access to one to one information.

Supporting teaching staff and planning the curriculum
Some nurses in independent schools are involved with teachers planning the PSHE/SRE curriculum. This will involve planning the topics to be covered, writing lesson plans, liaising with outside agencies and health services. Nurses should already have good contacts with outside agencies. The nursing press and study days often cover relevant issues. Training is available to enable the nurse to keep up to date with information on PSHE/SRE topics, which they can then pass on to teaching colleagues.

Teaching in a classroom setting

Many nurses in independent schools are willing to teach sessions as a part of the PSHE/SRE curriculum. The usual topics are menstruation, changes at puberty, contraception, sexually transmitted infections, sexuality, and issues such as how to say no to sex. They also cover other health topics. Teachers may feel that they do not have the knowledge to tackle these subjects, but the nurses may feel that they do not have the ability to teach, so a supportive role on both sides may well be advisable. Some nurses have completed a Cert. Ed. to enable them to fulfil this role effectively.

SRE Policy

Nurses in independent schools are in the ideal position to make a valuable input into the writing and reviewing of the school SRE policy.

Healthy Schools Scheme

In some independent schools, nurses have played a leading role in the implementation of this scheme. They should certainly be a part of the task group, as they have a valuable input to make, especially on the relevant health needs of the school.

Certificate of community nurses to support PSHE/SRE.

This new initiative is currently being piloted (April 2003). The aim is to provide a structured standards framework to enable community nurses to be recognised as PSHE/SRE specialists. Independent school nurses are in a good position to take part in this when it is rolled out in 2004.

A group of school nurses in the South West region have been keen to work alongside and support the school nurses that work in independent schools. A study/training day for all local independent school nurses was arranged through the 'adult health and reproductive services' (family planning). This training covered different aspects of young people's sexual health and included looking at curriculum planning for SRE. It was very popular and there are plans to repeat it.

A couple of independent schools have approached the school nursing service and requested teaching support for PSHE. Support has been provided in return for payment for the service – an arrangement that has worked for other services such as the family planning service. In terms of sustainability, the plan is to train up the schools' own nurses and to provide a forum where nurses can continue to meet up and support each other.

National Healthy School Standard – a whole school approach

> **'Sometimes I really miss my mum – I want to ask her about something and there is no-one else to ask.'**
> *Young woman aged 14 years*

SRE is part of a whole school approach to promoting the emotional health and well-being of children and young people. The NHSS emphasises the importance of such an approach. Children and young people learn from their experiences and observations as well as from lessons taught in the classroom. Even the very best PSHE and Citizenship which promotes health and well-being and a positive approach to diversity and difference, will not impact upon beliefs and behaviour if school systems, structures, experiences and expectations do not support classroom learning. What is seen and experienced in other classes, the playground and school corridors must be congruent with classroom learning if children and young people are to develop and grow with confidence and trust in adults. Positive, respectful and nurturing relationships among staff and pupils, between staff and staff, and pupils and pupils must be proactively fostered.

The NHSS identifies the following ten key elements for a whole school approach:

- leadership, management and managing change
- policy development
- curriculum planning and resourcing
- teaching and learning
- school culture and environment
- giving pupils a voice
- provision of pupil support services
- professional development, health and welfare of staff
- partnerships with parents, carers and local communities
- assessing, recording and reporting pupils' achievements.

A whole school approach is particularly important within the context of independent schools where pupils board. Unlike day pupils, they will not be able to have informal discussions with parents and carers and will have a different experience of privacy. Learning takes place both formally in SRE and informally through TV, magazines and peers. In 'boarding schools', house and other staff can helpfully identify informal opportunities to talk about relationships, for example following on from a television programme. All boarding facilities should provide information about local and national sources of support, including helplines.

Schools need a clear and consistent approach that all pupils and staff are confident with. For example, where SRE promotes the importance of asking for help and support, this assistance needs to be available within the school and to have effective links with the community services.

The four cornerstones of effective SRE

There are four cornerstones to the development of effective teaching about sex and relationships as part of PSHE and Citizenship (Blake, 2002). These are:

- participation of children and young people
- partnership with parents, carers and the wider community
- policy development
- practice, curriculum development and pastoral care.

The boxed section on pages 16 and 17 lists issues and questions which have proved helpful in developing effective teaching and learning in SRE.

The four cornerstones of effective SRE

Participation

For SRE to be relevant to the pupils they should be engaged in the development of policy and practice. There are a range of ways that pupils can be involved. They can

✔ become members of the healthy school or SRE policy development task group
✔ identify pupils' needs through surveys and interviews and collate this as part of the baseline data that informs policy and practice development
✔ become involved in the school council and the push for better SRE
✔ meet the Governors to discuss SRE
✔ become peer educators involved in delivering and supporting aspects of SRE

Policy

A policy on SRE needs to address and include

✔ information about the school and the process for policy development, including what efforts are to be made to communicate with parents/carers living abroad
✔ the aims of SRE
✔ what aspects will be covered, including reference to statutory requirements, good practice guidance and how it relates to school, local and national priorities as well as whole school issues related to SRE
✔ how it will be organised and covered
✔ how it will meet the needs of all pupils, including those who are marginalised and vulnerable or who need specific support
✔ who is responsible for coordinating and delivering SRE as part of PSHE and Citizenship and who is offering pastoral support
✔ the values framework for SRE within the school
✔ how pupil learning will be monitored and assessed
✔ how it links to other policies, including confidentiality, bullying and explicit expectations about sexual behaviour and relationships within the school
✔ how professional development needs will be identified and met
✔ how and when the policy will be monitored and reviewed

Partnerships

A number of partnerships need to be in place for the successful development and delivery of SRE. The groups and individuals brought together in this include

✔ children and young people (see Participation)
✔ parents/carers
✔ the wider community, including religious leaders
✔ Primary Care Trusts, the Local Education Authority, school health nurses, voluntary organisations
✔ local healthy schools programme
✔ local businesses (for example to sponsor activities or to provide work experience opportunities)
✔ local statutory and non-statutory agencies (e.g. for providing specialist resources, team teaching support)
✔ local coordinators such as Quality Protects coordinators and teenage pregnancy coordinators
✔ national organisations that provide advice, support, materials and information

Practice – Curriculum Development and Pastoral Care

The curriculum for SRE should be developed from the policy framework. The following issues need to be considered during curriculum development.

✔ Is the curriculum relevant to children's development?
✔ Does the curriculum enable pupils to develop core skills and values, including emotional resourcefulness?
✔ Are the objectives for each lesson clear and specific?
✔ Is the curriculum challenging for pupils?
✔ Are a range of teaching methods used that match with the aims and objectives and allow pupils to achieve at their own level?
✔ Does the curriculum build on prior learning? How is learning reinforced?
✔ How will pupil learning be monitored, assessed and progress recorded?
✔ Will outside visitors be involved and if so, how will you ensure the quality of the input?
✔ Are resources inclusive of all pupils?
✔ Will the classroom need rearranging to ensure a safe learning environment?
✔ How does SRE relate to other curriculum priorities such as ICT and literacy?
✔ Is it delivered by appropriately trained staff?
✔ Are there opportunities for emotional and social development across the whole curriculum and how is it coordinated?
✔ What pastoral support is available and how will pupils know they can get help about sex and relationships?
✔ How are links made to community services?

Policy

All schools need a PSHE and Citizenship policy so that everyone is clear about their roles and responsibilities and pupils, parents and carers are clear about their entitlement. The SRE Guidance (DfEE, 0116/2000) provides a framework which is as applicable to independent schools as those in the maintained sector. It recommends that SRE policy be developed within an overall policy on PSHE and Citizenship. This overall policy should in turn reflect and relate explicitly to other school policies, including those on child protection and confidentiality.

The following is an example of the information that should be included in a model PSHE and Citizenship policy.

The information to be included, ideally, in a PSHE and Citizenship policy

Introduction

> Name of school
> Date policy was completed
> People responsible for the policy
> Healthy school status

Background information

> A description of the school, including pupil roll, listing country of origin, ethnic and religious backgrounds, special needs
> A description of the development consultation process, including how pupils, parents, carers and the community are involved, and how national and local data is used to inform the curriculum

Policy statement

> A definition of PSHE and Citizenship
> A rationale for its provision
> How PSHE and Citizenship supports the core mission of the school and its values
> How the whole school ethos supports PSHE and Citizenship
> How the NHSS contributes to the effective delivery of PSHE and Citizenship

Organisation and planning

> Who is responsible for coordinating SRE/PSHE and Citizenship and who teaches it
> How pupils' needs are identified on a regular basis and how these will be responded to
> What extra provision there will be for people with particular needs, for example how the needs of children and young people with learning disabilities or sensory impairments, and of those more vulnerable to mental health, drug use or teenage pregnancy, will be met
> Where SRE is taught, whether in PSHE and Citizenship, in the wider curriculum, in special events and as a cross-curricular theme

Teaching methods and approaches
Criteria for resource selection
Resourcing and staff professional development

Assessment and reporting on learning

How learning is assessed, such as the ability to know and recognise feelings, the discovery of knowledge and skills and the development of a positive attitude to sexual health and well-being using self, peer and teacher learning

Pastoral systems and community services

How pupils will be made aware of pastoral services within the school, such as peer support schemes, school counsellors, tutorial systems, school health services (for example through posters, assemblies, lessons, Connexions personal advisors)
How pupils will be made aware of community services (for example, whether there will be health and youth service input to the curriculum, visits to services, mock clinics, and helplines including 'Sexwise')
What opportunities there are for help and support

Specific issues

Confidentiality and child protection
The involvement of outside visitors, parents, carers, voluntary agencies and peer educators
The process for approving and organising participation activities in the community

Monitoring and evaluation

How the implementation of the policy will be monitored
How the SRE policy will be evaluated and when it will be reviewed

Appendices

Specific issues such as: teaching about sex and relationships; promoting racial equality; religious and cultural aspects.

Participation

The involvement of pupils in the development and planning of SRE is essential if it is to meet their needs. A developing culture of consulting and involving young people is evident at government level; it is demonstrated in the publication of the *Core principles for consulting with and involving children and young people* (Children and Young People's Unit, 2001) and the development of young people's advisory forums, such as the groups advising the National Teenage Pregnancy Strategy, Quality Protects, and the Children and Young People's Unit. Under the Education Act 2002, local education authorities and governing bodies of maintained schools have to consult with pupils on decisions that affect them. Participation has been proven to be an effective part of school improvement strategies; it improves pupil and staff well-being and confidence through identifying the strengths of current practice, areas for improvement and strategies for making improvements (Hannam, 2001). From September 2004, schools will receive the Government Guidance on Participation which will expect them to involve pupils and young people in the life and development of the school; this will be helpful for the independent sector and will be available on the DfES website.

Pupils participate in the development of SRE by:

■ being part of policy and curriculum reviews, healthy school audits and planning activities
■ participating in structured opportunities to inform its content and approaches, such as draw and write sessions, whole group brainstorms
■ using anonymous question/comment boxes
■ discussing issues in the school and class councils
■ surveying other pupils' views on issues
■ researching local and national trends.

Partnerships

Partnerships really help to move things forward and contribute to policy review and development, classroom activities, the pool of knowledge and expertise on particular issues, and team teaching. Working in partnership across education, health and the voluntary sector has positive benefits for all concerned, which include:

■ producing a consistency of approach based on a shared values framework
■ sharing skills and expertise, so contributing to professional development
■ maximising human and financial resources by identifying the unique contributions of partners, including peers
■ providing links between the school and community services to improve access to services and inform the development of PSHE and Citizenship
■ developing support from parents and carers
■ providing opportunities for visitors to the classroom (including parents and carers) which enrich the curriculum
■ increasing intelligence on local issues, for example through school nurse health profiling or feedback from health professionals on local trends
■ providing information and support on meeting the needs of children with special health and educational needs, such as children in public care, disabled children and children from black and minority ethnic communities
■ developing joint educational and health objectives that can contribute to school improvement aims and public health priorities, such as teenage pregnancy and sexual health. For example, locally within education there may be a concern with boys' achievement, and within health a focus on working with boys as part of efforts to reduce teenage pregnancy. An activity to meet both of these strategic

objectives might include exploration of masculinity and gender issues within PSHE and Citizenship.

To be effective partnerships need to:

- be clear about the needs that have to be met
- be clear about the resources and expertise available locally
- be clear about the roles and responsibilities of individuals and organisations
- have clear and shared objectives that can be monitored against agreed indicators of success.

Key partners include:

- pupils
- parents and carers
- health personnel (including school and community nurses)
- Local Healthy Schools Partnerships
- local education authority advisory staff
- voluntary sector organisations
- police
- Connexions and learning mentors
- statutory sector agencies (social services, drug and alcohol teams).

Specific issues in developing SRE in independent schools

Consulting and involving parents and carers

It is established good practice to consult with children and young people and their parents and carers in the development and delivery of SRE. Consultation with parents and carers may be particularly difficult for some independent schools who fear it may be misinterpreted, and so raise needless anxiety and suggest there is cause for concern about sex and pregnancy in the school and, in some cases, parents and carers may not be near to hand or living in the country. Evidence shows parents and carers overwhelmingly support school-based SRE (NFER and HEA, 1994; Carrera and Ingham, 1998). Parents say that:

- there is a general lack of guidance for parents on how best to approach sex education at home
- they would like suggestions for appropriate books and booklets, especially visual materials, and other resources to use with their children
- they feel it is difficult to admit they don't always have a detailed knowledge about sex and relationships themselves
- they can feel threatened and deskilled when their children bring home information about sex and relationships and they are unable to discuss these issues comfortably
- they would like to be consulted and informed about the subjects being covered, the timing of provision and the style in which it is done.

Forming partnerships with parents and carers

- improves confidence in school-based SRE and helps parents and carers to understand the importance of SRE in children and young people's emotional and social development. It will also ensure they are confident SRE is developed within a positive values framework that respects different faith and cultural perspectives
- ensures effective home, school and community links so that parents and carers can reinforce learning within the home or care setting and community settings
- enhances the SRE curriculum when, for example, parents or carers are invited to talk about having or caring for a new baby in the family or share their relevant professional expertise. These talks must, of course, be tailored to fit the school values framework
- supports the development of parents' and carers' skills and confidence as well as enabling the school to offer them advice and guidance.

Some independent schools we have worked with have discovered innovative approaches for consulting with parents and carers. In one school, the parents association hosted a meeting where a visiting speaker had been invited to talk about SRE and answer questions. This was followed up by staff talking with parents and developing SRE. In another school, the parents were invited to attend a lunchtime meeting prior to picking up their children for the half-term holiday. Another school with weekly boarders held a series of meetings on Sunday evenings when parents and carers returned their children to school. For guidance on general principles and strategies for working with parents and carers, see the boxed section opposite.

Initial development

Effective staffing and timetabling

A recent report on SRE within maintained schools by OFSTED (2002) confirmed that SRE is best taught by a team of specialist, enthusiastic and well-trained teachers. Participants at the consultation event confirmed that this was also the case in independent schools. OFSTED also found that SRE is most effective when supported by a participative approach and positive ethos, delivered through a well-organised programme of PSHE and Citizenship and linked to other subjects and one-off activities, all of which are coordinated to ensure reinforcement and progression in learning. When planning SRE, the Qualifications and Curriculum Authority recommends that the school curriculum include:

- designated time, with support, for a specialist team of teachers who offer pupils structured and safe learning opportunities
- teaching about sex and relationships in PSHE and Citizenship and through other subject/curriculum areas. Some subjects, such as science, religious education and English, provide a useful focus for discussing some elements of SRE

- time allocated to occasional off-timetable experiences, such as 'health days', which provide a useful focus for an intensive study in SRE. These should form part of a carefully planned, ongoing PSHE and Citizenship curriculum. By involving pupils in planning these events, schools can offer positive opportunities for the development of planning and organisation skills, as well as building confidence in accessing community services.

General principles and strategies for working with parents and carers

- Support/consultation is best done as part of an ongoing process rather than, for example, as a one-off activity such as sending a letter informing parents and carers that sex education will be covered during the course of the academic year. Information sent nearer the time, and providing greater detail about content, will enable parents and carers to provide supplementary education at home and to answer any questions that their children might have.

- Where schools have little history of communication and dialogue with parents and carers, SRE is best covered within the broader context of consulting about PSHE and Citizenship, home/school liaison over health education, bullying and to talk about both sex and drug education.

- Make resources and books or booklists available to parents and carers to borrow and use.

- Use more than one forum for consulting and engaging with parents and carers. Some are happy and comfortable with an open evening or workshop, but others will prefer to be personally invited to contribute to a small discussion group or consulted on a specific issue, aspect of the programme or provision. You may need to go into the community too, rather than expect parents and carers to come to the school. Examples of approaches to consultation have included:
  - holding meetings when parents and carers are attending the school anyway for other meetings
  - accessing parents' and carers' views via newsletters, surveys or booklets
  - holding coffee mornings to provide an opportunity for parents and carers to talk to one another
  - running short courses to support parents and carers in talking to their children about sex and relationships which can be provided by local voluntary organisations or health promotion specialists
  - holding a meeting with parents and carers
  - inviting parents and carers into the classroom to support SRE
  - supporting parents and carers in talking to each other
  - ensuring that materials and support are available to parents and carers for whom English is not their first language.

Building staff skills and confidence
Staff delivering SRE need to feel confident to reflect on their own opinions and judgements, and work with sensitivity and understanding of children and young people's lives and experiences. Training and support is crucial and can be accessed

through a variety of sources, including the local healthy schools programme, Local Education Authority PSHE and Citizenship advisory teachers, and public health and health promotion teams within primary care trusts, as well as through national organisations and institutes of education. Teachers also benefit from team teaching with more experienced colleagues, school nurses or health promotion advisers.

The PSHE and Citizenship website for teachers (www.teachernet.gov.uk/pshe/) provides access to news, resources, information about training and events, professional development and support. It has a resource database, general information and a tool to assist professional development in PSHE.

The Wired For Health website (www.wiredforhealth.gov.uk) also provides support materials for teachers delivering SRE, as well as information and activities for children and young people. In 2003, a national scheme to provide training for teachers of PSHE will be rolled out through the NHSS. This will support the ongoing professional development of teachers via self-evaluation and a specialist module focusing on SRE.

Getting started

Planning initially involves auditing current provision and practice. The NHSS has designed a checklist to support schools in this process (DfES/DoH, 1999). The stages in the audit process are as follows:

- set up a task group that includes senior management, pupils, governors, parents/carers and relevant partners, for example school nurse or matron
- audit what the school is already doing – the NHSS and National Curriculum themes can be useful here
- identify gaps in provision
- set targets, taking account of key issues such as
  - inequalities and social inclusion issues
  - national and local priorities
  - legal requirements
  - relevant non-statutory guidance
- design the programme
- agree roles and responsibilities
- agree on methods for monitoring and evaluation
- identify staff professional development needs and plan accordingly.

Teaching and learning methods

Effective teaching methods maximise student learning by engaging children and young people in an active process of experiential learning (Kolb, 1984). Active learning methods have a built-in advantage over didactic methods as they offer (through their structure and process) automatic differentiation, so allowing for a range of attitudes to learning and abilities. They work by using creative processes to develop skills, acquire knowledge and explore beliefs and values. Active learning works primarily where children and young people work together. The group is a forum in which they learn from each other and practise using their knowledge and skills together as a group. The experience of listening to others' views and beliefs, practising skills, observing others and developing relationships supports effective learning.

The principle behind active learning lies in a sequence of different parts of the learning process, which are represented in the following diagram:

The processes involved in active learning

Do: This part of the process involves taking part in a structured activity, such as finding out some information, exploring beliefs and values or practising skills. Pupils could undertake, for example, a problem-solving or decision-making exercise, in which they are asked to decide a course of action that a young person might take. The following is an example of just such a case study.

Case Study
Jay and Dave have been invited to go drinking with his older brother. Jay wants to go. Dave doesn't because he thinks they might drink too much and have sex because they have been talking about it a lot. Jay is angry with Dave and keeps saying he is always trying to ruin any fun.

The case study has a series of questions such as:

- What might Dave be feeling?
- What might Dave be thinking?
- What might Dave do?
- What might be the consequences?
- What might Jay be feeling?
- What might Jay be thinking?
- What might Jay do?
- What might be the consequences?

This activity can be done in small groups. Each group works together to think about the answers to the questions. They then come together to share their ideas and practise how to deal with the situation before reflecting upon the activity, discussing their ideas and, where possible, agreeing the best way forward.

> **'We think that Dave should insist that they do not go because he does not want to get carried away or he should talk about his fears and plan not to drink too much.'**

Reflect: pupils are helped to reflect on the process through the use of open questions.

Teacher: *'What made you think that this was the right decision?'*
Pupils: *'We thought about the choices that are available and thought that the most important thing was that he did not do something he regretted afterwards.'*

Practising: by critically looking at how pupils reached their conclusions about what happened.

Teacher: *'So when you looked at the choices that were available to him how did you work out that what Dave wanted to do was more important? Did you think about the other options available to him? Did you think about the impact on Jay who wanted to go? How do you think Dave could respond to Jay's anger?'*

Pupil: *'Even though it might be difficult and Jay thinks it is a bit boring, Jay should think about Dave's concerns and they could try and find something else to do. Dave needs to stand his ground.'*

Teacher: *'How could Dave talk about this to Jay?'*

Pupil: *'He should tell her how he feels and make sure she knows that he is not boring and does want to have fun and try and make some suggestions about alternative things to do, or make sure they do not drink too much.'*

Learning and planning: at this stage the young people are encouraged to think about what has been learnt from the activity and how they might use this learning. The following gives an example of this.

Teacher: *'So, in either Jay's or Dave's situation in the future, what might someone do?'*

Pupil: *'Make sure that they talk to the other person and explain why they feel or think what they do. Really try to make sure they understand each other and think about other things they can do which are safe.'*

The following are useful teaching methods for facilitating this kind of learning.

■ **Quizzes and questionnaires:** These are useful for focusing on young people's knowledge or opinions about specific issues. They can also provide an assessment of future learning needs as well as trigger discussions.

- **Situation cards/scenarios:** This is where a specific situation is presented, providing a useful lead into discussions about values, attitudes and feelings.
- **Brainstorming:** This is when children or young people are invited to say or write down whatever comes to mind in relation to a word or thought. These can be helpful activities in triggering discussions and exploring ideas.
- **Art activities:** These might include poster making, painting and collage. Cutting out images from magazines or newspapers is particularly useful for looking at areas such as sexual stereotyping and body image, or for displaying information. These techniques can be particularly effective when used with children and young people who find it less easy or interesting to write. They can also help in building self-esteem, as the art can then be displayed.
- **Music:** This might involve writing a song or an advertising jingle. Music uses a range of skills and encourages cooperation in activities such as researching information, discussing attitudes and reaching a consensus. Again, there is a tangible result from this process.
- **Drama:** This might include role play or the use of puppets and masks. Drama is a useful distancing technique which allows young people to explore specific situations without revealing too much personal information. The 'freeze frame' technique where the action is 'frozen' and the participants discuss what has happened or will happen, is helpful to promote discussion.

For further information see the Forum Factsheet *Effective Learning* (see Appendix 1).

Group work

Effective group work is necessary for learning to take place. The climate in lessons should encourage creativity and allow pupils, either individually or as a group, to push the boundaries of their knowledge, explore and clarify their attitudes and values, and develop skills. Time taken to build the group and create a safe learning environment will pay dividends. For further information about effective group work see the Forum Factsheet *Effective Learning* (see Appendix 1).

Differentiated teaching

Differentiated teaching is important in meeting the needs of all pupils. Pupils will have different abilities based upon their emotional and physical development, life experiences, literacy levels and learning difficulties. Differentiated learning can be through:

- outcome – a task is set for all but each group can achieve it at their own level
- extension of activities – a group that has finished first can be given a further activity to increase their understanding
- support for the task – an extra adult such as a school nurse can work alongside the teacher
- resources – active learning techniques allow the teacher to manage more than one activity at a time
- grouping by ability – this may be by same level of ability or by mixed ability. For more information about differentiation in SRE see the Forum Factsheet *Taking the Initiative* (see Appendix 1).

Student review and assessment

Teachers will also need to assess pupils' learning in order to plan for future PSHE and Citizenship. Teachers can help pupils assess and review their learning, as part of the learning process, by asking them to consider the following questions.

- What new information did I learn?
- What new skills did I practise?
- What do I now understand?
- I can use what I learnt today when …?
- I now feel confident about …?
- I can resolve conflict or handle differences by …?
- How can my assumptions or prejudices affect other people?
- What else do I need to learn to feel confident about …?

Teachers can gather evidence of student learning through a variety of methods, including:

- self-assessment (checklist, diary, display or questionnaire)
- peer assessment (observation of role play, checklist, interviewing each other about participation activities, video or audio tapes)
- whole group assessment (brainstorms, graffiti sheets, worksheets, role play and drama, completing sentence stems)
- teacher assessment (checklist, written records, response to group work activity)
- joint teacher and pupil assessment (reflection on involvement in school or community activities and ability to work within the group)
- other adult assessment (through work experience reports, teaching assistant and learning mentor assessment, external award systems).

Although there are no statutory assessment requirements for SRE, schools should keep records on all aspects of pupils' development and achievement. Annual school reports should include a section on PSHE and Citizenship.

Teachers' evaluation

Teachers evaluate their teaching practice in order to establish the effectiveness of their lessons in meeting their objectives, identify professional development needs, and adapt and change SRE to meet the needs of pupils. This evaluation can happen through a natural process, or be aided by questionnaire surveys of pupils or discussion. Some useful questions to consider are:

- What feedback did I get from the pupils?
- Did the aims and objectives of the lesson/programme meet the needs of the pupils?
- What did I do well?
- Did the methods facilitate learning?
- Did the resources facilitate learning?
- What would I do differently next time?

Suggested learning objectives

In its recent report on SRE provision in maintained schools, OFSTED noted that assessment of learning is an area for development in many schools. To support teachers in planning and assessing SRE provision, OFSTED provided a list of suggested learning objectives organised by key stage (see boxed sections below).

These learning objectives are incredibly useful in terms of knowledge and understanding as well as values clarification. However, SRE is further strengthened by helping children and young people develop skills in areas such as:

- asking for and offering help
- identifying and naming emotions
- being a good friend
- listening
- giving an opinion
- accessing services
- negotiating
- decision making
- forgiving
- being empathic
- critical thinking
- using a condom and contraception effectively.

By the end of Key Stage 1

Pupils will be able to:
- recognise and compare the main external parts of the bodies of humans*
- recognise similarities and differences between themselves and others and treat others with sensitivity*
- identify and share feelings with others
- recognise safe and unsafe situations
- identify and be able to talk to someone they trust
- be aware that their feelings and actions have an impact on others
- make a friend, talk with them and share feelings
- use simple rules for dealing with strangers and for resisting pressure when they feel uncomfortable or at risk.

Pupils will know and understand:
- that animals, including humans, grow and reproduce*
- that humans and animals can produce offspring and these grow into adults*
- the basic rules for keeping themselves safe and healthy
- about safe places to play and safe people to be with
- the needs of babies and young people
- ways in which they are like and different from others
- that they have some control over their actions and beliefs
- the names of the main external parts of the body including agreed names for the sexual parts
- why families are special for caring and sharing.

Pupils will have considered:
- why families are special
- the similarities and differences between people
- how their feelings and actions have an impact on other people.

*Part of the National Curriculum for science.

By the end of Key Stage 2

Pupils will be able to:
- express opinions, for example, about relationships and bullying
- listen to and support others
- respect other people's viewpoints and beliefs
- recognise their changing emotions with friends and family and be able to express their feelings positively
- identify adults they can trust and who they can ask for help
- be self-confident in a wide range of new situations, such as seeking new friends
- form opinions that they can articulate to a variety of audiences
- recognise their own worth and identify positive things about themselves
- balance the stresses of life in order to promote both their own mental health and well-being and that of others
- see things from other people's viewpoints, for example their parents and their carers
- discuss moral issues
- listen and support their friends and manage friendship problems
- recognise and challenge stereotypes, for example in relation to gender
- recognise the pressure of unwanted physical contact, and know ways of resisting it.

Pupils will know and understand:
- that the life processes common to humans and other animals include growth and reproduction*
- about the main stages of human life*
- that safe routines can stop the spread of viruses including HIV
- about the physical changes that take place at puberty, why they happen and how to manage them
- the many relationships in which they are involved
- where individual families and groups can find help
- how the media impact on forming attitudes
- about keeping themselves safe when involved in risky activities
- that their actions have consequences and be able to anticipate the results of them
- about different forms of bullying people and the feelings of both bullies and victims
- why being different can provoke bullying and know why this is unacceptable
- about, and accept, a wide range of different family arrangements, for example, second marriages, fostering, extended families and three or more generations living together.

Pupils will have considered:
- the diversity of lifestyles
- others' points of view, including their parents' or carers'

- why being different can provoke bullying and why this is unacceptable
- when it is appropriate to take a risk and when to say no and seek help
- the diversity of values and customs in the school and in the community
- the need for trust and love in established relationships.

* Part of the National Curriculum for science.

By the end of Key Stage 3

Pupils will be able to:
- manage changing relationships
- recognise the risk to personal safety in sexual behaviour and be able to make safe decisions
- ask for help and support
- explain the relationship between their self-esteem and how they see themselves
- develop skills of assertiveness in order to resist peer pressure and stereotyping
- see the complexity of moral, social and cultural issues and be able to form a view of their own
- develop good interpersonal skills to sustain existing relationships as they grow and change and to help them make new relationships
- develop empathy with the core values of family life in all its variety of forms
- recognise the need for commitment, trust and love in meaningful relationships which may manifest themselves in a variety of forms, including marriage
- recognise the stages of emotions in relation to loss and change caused by divorce, separation and new family members and how to manage their feelings positively.

Pupils will know and understand:
- that fertilisation in humans is the fusion of a male and a female cell*
- the physical and emotional changes that take place during adolescence*
- about the human reproductive system, including the menstrual cycle and fertilisation*
- how the foetus develops in the uterus*
- how the growth and reproduction of bacteria and replication of viruses can affect health*
- how the media influence understanding and the attitudes towards sexual health
- how good relationships can promote mental well-being
- the law relating to sexual behaviour of young people
- the sources of advice and support
- about when and where to get help, such as at a genito-urinary medicine clinic.

Pupils will have considered:
- the benefits of sexual behaviour within a committed relationship
- how they see themselves affects their self-confidence and behaviour
- the importance of respecting difference in relation to gender and sexuality
- how it feels to be different and be discriminated against
- issues such as the costs of early sexual activity
- the unacceptability of prejudice and homophobic bullying
- what rights and responsibilities mean in relationships.

* Part of the National Curriculum for science.

By the end of Key Stage 4

Pupils will be able to:
- recognise the influences and pressures around sexual behaviour and respond appropriately and confidently seek professional health advice
- manage emotions associated with changing relationships with parents and friends
- see both sides of an argument and express and justify a personal opinion
- have the determination to stand up for their beliefs and values
- make informed choices about the pattern of their lifestyle which promotes well-being
- have the confidence to assert themselves and challenge offending behaviour
- develop qualities of empathy and sympathy and the ability to respond emotionally to the range and depth of feelings within close relationships
- work cooperatively with a range of people who are different from themselves.

Pupils will know and understand:
- the ways in which hormonal control occurs, including the effects of the sex hormones and some medical uses of hormones including the control and promotion of fertility*
- the defence mechanisms of the body*
- how sex is determined in humans*
- how HIV and other STIs affect the body
- the link between eating disorders and self-image and sexual identity
- the risks of early sexual activity and the link with the use of alcohol
- how the different forms of contraception work and where to get advice
- the role of statutory and voluntary organisations
- the law in relation to sexual activity for young people and adults
- how their own sexual identity is influenced by both their personal values and those of their family and society
- how to respond appropriately within a range of social relationships
- how to access the statutory and voluntary agencies which support relationships in crisis
- the qualities of good parenting and its value to family life
- the benefits of marriage or a stable partnership in bringing up children
- the way different forms of relationships including marriage depend for their success on maturity and commitment.

Pupils will have considered:
- their developing sense of sexual identity and feel confident and comfortable with it
- how personal, family and social values influence behaviour
- the arguments around moral issues such as abortion, contraception and the age of consent
- the individual contributions made by partners in a sustained relationship and how these can be of joy or benefit to both
- the consequences of close relationships including having children and how this will create family ties which impact on their lives and those of others.

*Part of the National Curriculum for science.

Involving outside organisations and individuals

Using outside visitors
A range of visitors can support SRE. Visitors should form part of a planned programme. Visitors can enhance SRE by providing expertise, a link to services and community support.

One school for boys invited a community worker to work with a group of 12 year olds. Prior to the session the boys were asked to write down any questions and post them in a sealed container. These then formed the basis of a question and answer session and more in-depth work around assertiveness and relationships which the boys identified as their most important concern.

Building the links with sexual health and other services
SRE should ensure that children and young people are informed about and supported in accessing individual advice and support as and when they need it. In some cases this support may be available within the school through school nurses or other professionals. In others, this may not be available and, even where it is, children and young people may want to seek advice, care or treatment from specialist agencies outside the school. Through forging closer links with local services, schools can not only support children and young people but also access expertise and accurate information about their needs which can then be used to enhance programmes of SRE. As a minimum, all schools with secondary aged pupils should be providing them with information about sexual health services that are available within the community. School staff can provide information through SRE, display leaflets and contact information for services. Involving local service providers in SRE as external visitors can help promote awareness, knowledge and confidence about accessing services among children and young people. Schools may also wish to incorporate visits to services as part of planned SRE. In some cases schools may choose to develop partnerships with local services to improve access. Further information is available in *Secondary Schools and Sexual Health Services: Forging the Links* (Thistle, 2003, see Appendix 1).

Specific needs of pupils

Providing SRE for pupils with physical and learning disabilities and special needs
Sex and relationships education is an important part of the curriculum for all young people, and young disabled people and those with special needs are no exception. However, disabled children and young people, and those with special needs are less likely to receive sex education in school and at home. In addition, their experiences are often excluded or misrepresented in the media and in SRE resources.

For children and young people with a disability, SRE takes into account specific needs, develops appropriate methods of teaching and learning, and uses relevant resources and materials. Children and young people with disabilities are in need of special attention because of:

- their vulnerability to prejudice, discrimination and sexual abuse
- the lack of opportunities available to them to develop, for example, interpersonal skills
- a lack of opportunities to make and sustain friendships and develop intimate relationships
- the lack of appropriate sexual health education and support
- the lack of accessible services and adequately trained staff
- the lack of appropriate resources for people with a range of physical, learning and sensory impairments.

High quality SRE contributes to reducing these inequalities. A key area that disabled children and young people, and those with special needs, feel should be covered in SRE, is the (largely negative) impact on their relationships of society's attitudes towards disability, special needs and sexuality.

Children and young people with disabilities are a diverse group and there is a need to think creatively in responding to the range of disabilities, impairments and special needs that they may have. For example, those with a learning disability may require particular support in relation to issues of 'public and private', while those with a visual impairment may need to be able to touch and feel objects, such as model penises. Those children and young people with a physical disability that requires intimate care, may need particular help and support in claiming a sense of rights over their own bodies.

For more information see the Forum Factsheet *Ensuring Entitlement: Sex and relationships education for disabled children* (see Appendix 1). There is also a chapter on providing SRE for children and young people with learning disabilities in *Sex and Relationships Education: A step by step guide for teachers* (Blake, 2002).

Working in single-sex settings
Some independent schools are single-sex. In this context, SRE should address both the specific needs of the pupils in the school, be they boys or girls, and provide pupils with insight and a balanced view on the issues, needs and concerns of the opposite sex.

Working with young women

> **'You've got no idea the types of pressure we are under to get it all right including relationships.'**
> *Young woman aged 15 years*

While girls may be exposed to more sources of information about sex – family, friends and magazines, for example – they tell us that their formal and informal sex education is not relevant to their needs. Furthermore, young lesbians, young women from minority ethnic groups and young disabled women report more limited access to this kind of information. There is a new assumption that girls are full of confidence, out-achieving boys academically, in short that 'girl-power' has arrived. However, many young women suffer chronic low self-esteem and poor body image, and put up with unsatisfactory or unsafe sex, or having sex which they later regret. SRE with girls and young women should deal explicitly with the links between self-image, confidence and self-esteem, and managing sex and relationships.

For more information about working with girls and young women see the Forum Factsheet *Meeting the needs of girls and young women in sex and relationships education* (see Appendix 1).

Working with young men

> **'My dad went to a boarding school and he sent me and he expects me to be like him.'**
> **Young man aged 14 years**

> **'The really *really* important thing missing for these boys is chances to communicate and be with girls. We try to make sure we help them to understand and respect girls.'**
> **Teacher at an all boys school**

Boys have tended to get less sex education than girls within the family and to have talked less about sex with other informed sources such as health professionals. Boys may actively seek and glean information from each other and a variety of sources, such as the internet, which can lead to inaccurate and partial knowledge and increased anxieties. Boys may perceive themselves to be under pressure to be sexually experienced and knowledgeable in order to maintain status in their male peer group and to avoid being bullied. The resultant macho posturing, which many teachers experience as disruptive and discouraging, really reflects the gap between the public and private faces of masculinity. Good SRE with young men will address these pressures to 'act like man' and enable boys and young men to express their anxieties and concerns.

For more information about working with boys and young men see the Forum Factsheet *Meeting the needs of boys and young men in sex and relationships education* (see Appendix 1).

Meeting the needs of young gay men and lesbian women
Growing up lesbian or gay can be a frightening and lonely experience. Many young people experience bullying and rejection by their peers and adults (Forrest, Biddle and Clift, 1997; Lenderyou and Ray, 1997). A national survey of homophobic bullying and violence showed that name-calling and harassment was common and that half of all violent physical attacks on young lesbian and gay people took place in school (Mason and Palmer, 1996). It is important not to separate homosexuality from the rest of SRE by dealing with it in one lesson or ignoring it completely. This gives the impression that heterosexual and homosexual relationships and experiences are innately different. Explicit lessons in which prejudice and discrimination are explored are helpful but discussion about different sexualities should be integrated throughout SRE. Ensuring that the word 'partner' is used rather than 'boyfriend' or 'girlfriend' can affirm and

validate rather than exclude young lesbian and gay people. In addition to providing SRE, which is sensitive to and inclusive of different sexualities, schools need to make sure that young lesbians and gay people can access information and support which is specifically relevant to them. This can be done through the school or by providing links to relevant organisations in the wider community.

Ethnicity, faith and culture

Good SRE is sensitive to and mindful of different cultures and faiths. Pupils with a faith or cultural tradition need to feel that SRE affirms and respects their beliefs and values. All pupils also need to be supported in developing their understanding of the diversity of lifestyles, beliefs and practices and a respect for the differences between people. The Race Relations Act 2000 requires all schools to work towards promoting race equality. Schools are required to create an environment and provide a curriculum that are relevant to all pupils and promotes racial harmony. Children and young people from some black and minority ethnic groups often face implicit and explicit racism and experience sexual ill health (for example HIV infection disproportionately affects African communities). SRE provides an opportunity to explore different cultural values and beliefs, and so resources need to be representative of different races and cultures.

For further information see *Faith, Values and Sex and Relationships Education* (Blake and Katrak, 2002).

Part 3: **Working with the independent sector**

This section is for professionals in education and health working with, or wanting to work with, schools in the independent sector. It offers ideas, strategies and examples of ways in which people have successfully engaged with independent schools. It draws on the experiences and ideas of participants at the consultation event.

The National Healthy School Standard and independent schools

The NHSS requires that all local programmes have a strategy for recruiting all schools, including those in the independent sector. Independent schools, as a minimum, should be receiving relevant newsletters and information, and may, depending on the population, require specific and targeted help and support.

Positive strategies for working with independent schools to develop SRE

The following eight key strategies provide positive steps in the development of SRE in independent schools.

1. Funding
Some colleagues working within healthy schools programmes are unclear about whether they can offer services to independent schools without charging. While it is clear that Standards funding is not to be used to support work in independent schools, primary care trusts have a remit to support the health of all their residents. They may therefore choose to offer support to independent schools without charging.

Where it is not possible to offer a free service, it is important that professionals supporting schools are clear about the services they can offer, the expected outcomes of these services and the cost. Colleagues in independent schools confirmed it is not always necessary to offer a free service but it is always necessary to be clear about value for money.

2. Talking about sex and relationships education

When engaging with the independent sector, be clear and confident about the rationale for developing SRE based on the following:

- the expressed views and needs of children and young people
- an understanding of the increased role of the school in supporting children and young people's pastoral needs when living away from home
- an understanding of the context in which SRE may be delivered, for example informally by the house staff as well as in formal SRE lessons
- a commitment to children and young people's educational entitlement to high quality SRE
- evidence of local and national trends and priorities
- an understanding of SRE's contribution to school improvement and meeting public health priorities.

Utilising this rationale can help schools see the positive benefits of SRE and reflect these in turn to parents and carers.

3. Ensuring inclusion on mailing lists

At the consultation event we explicitly asked colleagues working in independent schools to offer ideas about how to improve SRE. One responded, 'For a start, you could put us on the mailing lists!' All local healthy schools programmes should, as a minimum, ensure that independent schools get information about the local programme through newsletters and mail outs.

Some local areas have network meetings focusing on either PSHE and Citizenship or SRE specifically. Independent schools could be invited to these events in order to benefit from local skills and expertise.

4. Identifying a named person within the school

Before sending information or resources to an independent school it is important to identify a named person. A PSHE coordinator is preferable, although an alternative might be someone who takes a lead in pastoral care.

If information is sent 'cold' to the head teacher it is unlikely that it will find its way to the appropriate person. If you are unable to identify a named person within the school prior to sending information, address the letter to the 'Head of PSHE and Citizenship' (not coordinator) as this implies status and importance.

5. Making contact with independent schools

As with all schools, independent schools receive vast amounts of paperwork through the post. If SRE is not a priority it is unlikely that 'cold' mailings will encourage staff within the schools to take action, particularly if the sender of the letter is unknown. Positive strategies for making contact include:

- explicitly stating that the training, resource or meeting is relevant for independent school staff

- following up mailings with a phone call to develop a trusting relationship
- offering to meet personally to discuss issues raised in the mailing
- ensuring that the letter is clear about the help available and is focused and specific
- targeting mailings so that they are relevant to the staff that receives them. For example, in a boarding school information often goes to a head of house rather than to teaching staff. If you are unsure to whom you need to write, include a sentence asking for the mailing to be forwarded to relevant teaching staff or care staff
- find a person already trusted by the school to act as a conduit. For example, most independent schools have a school nurse or use outside organisations. Encourage them, as somebody who already has a positive relationship, to arrange a meeting or recommend attendance at a training course.

6. Involving a person on the healthy schools partnership group

One colleague who attended the consultation event sits on the local healthy schools partnership group. He does not explicitly represent the independent sector. However, being a part of the group has enabled him to work with local colleagues to ensure that the programme considers the independent sector in their decisions.

This does not mean that the programme always decides to offer equal support to the maintained and independent sectors, but there is always a clear rationale for what is and what is not offered.

7. Make contact with the school nurse

Many independent schools have a school nurse responsible for the health and well-being of pupils. Make contact with the nurse to discuss possible formal and informal opportunities for sex and relationships education.

8. Forming partnerships with the maintained sector

The DfES is committed to providing opportunities for independent and maintained schools to come together and learn from each other.

Appendix 1: **Useful resources**

Key government documents and resources

Department for Education and Employment (2000) *Sex and Relationship Education Guidance* (0116/2000)

Department for Education and Employment and Qualifications and Curriculum Authority (1999) *The National Curriculum Handbook for Primary School Teachers in England*

Department for Education and Employment and Qualifications and Curriculum Authority (1999) *The National Curriculum Handbook for Secondary School Teachers in England*

Department of Health and Department for Education and Employment (1999) *National Healthy School Standard: Guidance*

Department of Health and Department for Education and Employment (1999) *National Healthy School Standard: Getting Started*

Department of Health and Department for Education and Employment (2000) *National Healthy School Standard: Sex and relationships education (SRE)*

Qualifications and Curriculum Authority (2000) *Personal, Social and Health Education and Citizenship at Key Stages One and Two. Initial guidance for schools*

Qualifications and Curriculum Authority (2000) *Personal, Social and Health Education at Key Stages Three or Four. Initial guidance for schools*

Qualifications and Curriculum Authority (2000) *Citizenship Education at Key Stages Three or Four. Initial guidance for schools*

Qualifications and Curriculum Authority (2001) *Personal, Social and Health Education and Citizenship: Teaching and assessing the curriculum for pupils with learning difficulties*

Sex Education Forum resources

All of the following resources are available from the National Children's Bureau, either phone 020 7843 6000 or go to the NCB online bookshop at www.ncb-books.org.uk

Blake, S (2001) *Sex and Relationships Education curriculum resources for Key Stages 3 and 4 PSHE and Citizenship.* Award Scheme Development Accreditation Network / Sex Education Forum / National Children's Bureau

Blake, S (2002) *Sex and Relationships Education – a step by step guide for teachers.* David Fulton Publishers

Blake, S and Frances, G (2001) *Just Say No! To abstinence education, Lessons learnt from a sex education study tour to the United States.* Sex Education Forum and National Children's Bureau

Blake, S and Katrak, Z (2002) *Faith, Values and Sex and Relationships Education.* Sex Education Forum

Blake, S and Katrak, Z (2003 forthcoming) *Ethnicity, culture and sex and relationships education*. Sex Education Forum

Lenderyou, G and Ray, C eds (1997) *Let's Hear it for the Boys! Supporting Sex and Relationships Education for boys and young men.* Sex Education Forum

Patel-Kanwal, H and Frances-Lenderyou, G (1998) *Let's talk about sex and relationships: A policy and practice framework for working with children and young people in public care.* Sex Education Forum

Royal National Institute for the Blind and Health Education Authority and Sex Education Forum (2000) *Sexual Health Resources for working with children and young people who are visually impaired and blind*

Scott, L (1996) *Partnership with Parents in sex education: A guide for schools and those working with them*. Sex Education Forum

Sex Education Forum (2002) *Sex, myths and education. Young people talking about sex and relationships education. A video resource*. Sex Education Forum and National Children's Bureau and The Kosh

Sense Interactive CDs (2003) *Sense, sex and relationships*. An interactive Cd for 14- to 16-year-olds. Sense interactive CDs and NCB

Thistle, S (2003 forthcoming) *Secondary Schools and Sexual Health Services: Forging the Links*. Sex Education Forum.

The Sex Education Forum produces a range of four and eight page factsheets which are designed to offer accessible and practical digests of current research and ideas. Each fact-sheet focuses on a specific aspect of SRE. For a full list of titles contact the Sex Education

Forum on 020 7843 6056 or visit the website www.ncb.org.uk/sef and download them for free.

Current Factsheets available from the Sex Education Forum and NCB include:
Meeting the needs of boys and young men in sex and relationships education (1997)

Effective Learning: Approaches to teaching sex education (1997)

The Framework for Sex and Relationships Education (1999)

Meeting the needs of girls and young women in sex and relationships education (2000)

Taking the Initiative: Positive Guidance on sex and relationships education in the secondary school (2000)

Ensuring Entitlement: Sex and Relationships Education for Disabled Children (2001)

PSHE and Citizenship – ensuring effective sex and relationships education (2001)

Sex and Relationships Education in the Primary School (2002)

Developing a whole school approach to PSHE and Citizenship (2003)

Useful organisations

AVERT
4 Brighton Road, Horsham, West Sussex RH13 5BA.
Tel: 0140 321 0202 Website: www.avert.org
Avert is an international HIV and AIDS charity. It provides online statistics, resources and other information about HIV and AIDS for young people and professionals.

Brook
Unit 421, Highgate Studios, London NW5 1TL.
Tel: 020 7284 6040 Website: www.brook.org.uk
Brook publishes a range of resources for young people and professionals.

Centre for HIV and Sexual Health
22 Collegiate Crescent, Sheffield S10 2BA.
Tel: 0114 226 1900 Website: www.sexualhealthsheffield.co.uk
The centre provides local and national training, consultancy, and produces a wide range of leaflets and publications.

FPA
2–12 Pentonville Road, London N1 9FP.
Tel: 020 7837 5432 Website: www.fpa.org.uk
FPA offers training and consultancy as well as resources for children, young people and professionals.

Image in Action
Chinnor Road, Bledlow Ridge, High Wycombe, HP14 4AG.
Tel: 0149 448 1632
Image in Action works with young people with learning disabilities using drama, group work and active learning to teach sex education. It offers consultancy, training and resources.

Local Support
The LEA advisory team healthy schools programmemay be able to offer support. There will generally be a charge.

Your local Teenage Pregnancy Coordinator can offer information on local services, local voluntary organisations and other health professionals who can contribute to SRE. The website www.teenagepregnancyunit.gov.uk provides a list of local coordinators.

NAPCE (National Association for Pastoral Care in Education)
c/o Institute of Education, The University of Warwick, Westwood, Coventry CV4 7AL.
Tel: 0247 6523810 Website: www.warwick.ac.uk/wie/napce
NAPCE publishes *Pastoral Care in Education.*

National Healthy School Standard Team
The NHSS produces support materials on different aspects of PSHE and Citizenship. You can find these materials on, and contact your local healthy school coordinator through, the website www.wiredforhealth.gov.uk

Relate
Herbert Gray College, Little Church Street, Rugby, Warwickshire CV21 3AP.
Tel: 0845 456 1310 Website: www.relate.org.uk
Relate provides counselling, training and publications.

Sex Education Forum
c/o National Children's Bureau, 8 Wakley Street, London EC1V 7QE.
Tel: 020 7843 6052 E-mail: sexedforum@ncb.org.uk Website: www.ncb.org.uk/sef
The Forum is the national authority on SRE. It produces a series of factsheets and publications and maintains lists of useful teaching resources on its website.

TeacherNet
Website: www.teachernet.gov.uk/pshe
Teachernet is a dedicated learning and development resource for teachers of PSHE and Citizenship. It is designed for experienced and new PSHE teachers alike. It contains a flexible, interactive tool to help identify your development needs; a signpost to 'learning pathways'; a database of resources; and the opportunity to share ideas, seek advice and contribute good practice through the bulletin board

UK Independent Schools Website
Website: www.uk-independent-schools.co.uk
For links to all the sites concerning UK independent schools.

The Independent Schools Council
Independent Schools Council, Grosvenor Gardens House, 35–37 Grosvenor Gardens,
London SW1W 0BS.
Tel: 020 7798 1500 Fax: 020 7798 1591 E-mail: isc@iscis.uk.net
Web: www.iscis.uk.net

Members of the Independent Schools Council
The Governing Bodies Association (GBA)
The Governing Bodies of Girls Schools Association (GBGSA)
The Incorporated Association of Preparatory Schools (IAPS)
The Independent Schools Association (ISA)
The Headmasters and Headmistresses Conference (HMC)
The Girls School Association (GSA)
The Society of Headmasters and Headmistresses of Independent Schools (SHMIS)
The Independent Schools Bursars Association (BSA)

See entry for UK Independent Schools Website for web address linking to websites of
above members.

The Independent Schools Information Service (ISIS)
5 Tolethorpe Close, Burley Grange, Oakham, LE15 6JF
Tel: 01572 722 726 E-mail: central@isis.org.uk Website: www.isuk.org.uk

Members of the Sex Education Forum

Members of the Sex Education Forum are national organisations involved in providing or
supporting sex education. Members have agreed a consensus statement The Framework for
Sex and Relationships Education (www.ncb.org.uk/sef). The Forum works together to
ensure all children and young people's entitlement to good quality sex and relationships
education.

ACET	www.acetuk.org
APAUSE	www.ex.ac.uk/sshs/apause
Association for Health Education Co-ordinators (ASHEC)	Not available
AVERT	www.avert.org.uk
Barnardos	www.barnardos.org.uk
Black Health Agency (BHA)	Blackhealthagency.org.uk (under construction)
British Humanist Association	www.humanism.org.uk
Brook Advisory Centres	www.brook.org.uk
Catholic Education Service	www.catholiceducation.org.uk

Centre for HIV and Sexual Health	www.sexualhealthsheffield.co.uk
Childline	www.childline.org.uk
The Children's Society	www.the-childrens-society.org.uk
Church of England Board of Education	www.natsoc.org.uk
Community Practitioners and Health	
Visitors Association (CPHVA)	www.msfcphva.org
Education for Choice	www.efc.org.uk
Families and Friends of Lesbians and Gays (FFLAG)	www.fflag.org.uk
Forward	
fpa	www.fpa.org.uk
Girlguiding UK	www.guides.org.uk
Image in Action	Not available
Jewish Marriage Council	www.jmc-uk.org
League of Jewish Women	Not available
Lesbian and Gay Christian Movement (LGCM)	www.lgcm.org.uk
Marriage Care	www.marriage.org.uk
Medical Foundation for AIDS and Sexual Health	www.medfash.org.uk
MENCAP	www.mencap.org.uk
The Methodist Church	www.methodist.org.uk
The Mother's Union	www.themothersunion.org.uk
National AIDS Trust (NAT)	www.nat.org.uk
National Association for Governors and	
Managers (NAGME)	www.nagme.org.uk
National Association for Pastoral Care in	
Education (NAPCE)	www.warwick.ac.uk/wie/napce
National Children's Bureau (NCB)	www.ncb.org.uk
National Council of Women of Great Britain	www.ncqgb.org.uk
National Health Education Group (NHEG)	www.nheg.org.uk
National Society for the Prevention of Cruelty	
to Children (NSPCC)	www.nspcc.org.uk
National Youth Agency	www.nya.org.uk
NAZ Project London	www.naz.org.uk
NCH	www.nch.org.uk
NSCOPSE	Not available
One Plus One	www.oneplusone.org.uk
Parenting Education and Support Forum	www.parenting-forum.org.uk
RELATE	www.relate.org.uk
Royal College of Nursing	www.rcn.org.uk
Save the Children Fund	www.savethechildren.org.uk
Society for Health Promotion Officers and Personal	
Relationships of People with a Disability	www.spod-uk.org.uk
Society of Health Advisors in STD (SHASTD)	www.shastd.org.uk
TACADE	www.tacade.com
Terrence Higgins Trust	www.tht.org.uk

Trust for the Study of Adolescence (TSA)
Working With Men
YWCA

www.tsa.uk.com
www.workingwithmen.org
www.ywca-gb.org.uk

Appendix 2: **References**

Blake, S (2002) *Sex and Relationships Education: A step by step guide for teachers*. David Fulton Publishers

Blake, S and Katrak, Z (2002) *Faith, Values and Sex and Relationships Education.* Sex Education Forum

Carrera, C and Ingham, R (1998) Liaison between parents and schools on sex education policies: Identifying some gaps. *Sex Education Matters*, 15, 11–12

Children and Young People's Unit (2001) *Learning to Listen: Core principles for involving children and young people*. Children and Young People's Unit

Collins, J and others (2002) Programs-That-Work: CDC's guide to effective programs that reduce health-risk behaviour or youth. *Journal of School Health,* 72, 3, 93–9

Department for Education and Employment (1999) *National Healthy School Standard Guidance.* Department for Education and Employment

Department for Education and Employment (2000) *Sex and Relationships Guidance*. Department for Education and Employment

Department for Education and Employment and Department of Health (1999) *National Healthy School Standard guidance: getting started – a guide for schools*. Department for Education and Employment and Department of Health

Department of Health (2001) *The National Strategy for Sexual Health and HIV*. Department of Health

Department of Health (2002) *Government response to the first annual report of the independent advisory group on teenage pregnancy*. Department of Health

Forrest, S and Biddle, G and Clift, S (1997) *Talking about Homosexuality in the Secondary School*. AVERT

Hannam, D (2001) *A pilot study to evaluate the impact of the student participation aspects of the citizenship order on standards in secondary school.* Department for Education and Skills

Health Education Authority (1998) *Reducing the rate of teenage pregnancies: an overview of the effectiveness of interventions and programmes aimed at reducing unintended conceptions in young people*. Health Education Authority

Independent Schools Information Service (2001) *Central England schools handbook.* Independent Schools Information Service

Kolb, DA (1984) *Experiential learning: experience as the source of learning and development*. Prentice-Hall

Lenderyou, G and Ray, C eds (1997) *Let's Hear It for the Boys: Supporting SRE for boys and young men.* Sex Education Forum

Mason, A and Palmer, A (1996) *Queerbashing: A Survey of Hate Crimes against Gay Men and Lesbians.* Stonewall

National Foundation for Education Research and Heath Education Authority (1994) *Parents, schools and sex education*. National Foundation for Education Research and Health Education Authority

OFSTED (2002) *Sex and relationships*. Office for Standards in Education

Public Health Laboratory Service (2001) *Diagnoses of selected sexually transmitted infections (STIs) in GUM clinics: England, Wales and Northern Ireland 1996–2001 (provisional data for 2001).* Public Health Laboratory Service

Qualifications and Curriculum Authority and Department for Education and Employment (1999) *The National Curriculum*. Qualifications and Curriculum Authority and Department for Education and Employment

Race Relations Amendment Act (2000). Chapter 34. Stationery Officer

Rivers, K and others (1999) *Learning Lessons: A report on two research studies informing the National Healthy School Standard*. DoH/DfEE

Sex Education Forum (1999a) *The framework for sex and relationships education*. Sex Education Forum

Sex Education Forum (1999b) *Forum factsheet 18: Supporting parents in sex and relationships education*. Sex Education Forum

Social Exclusion Unit (1999) *Teenage Pregnancy*. The Cabinet Office

Wellings, K and others (2001) Sexual behaviour in Britain: Early heterosexual experience, *The Lancet* (358) 1843–1850

Wight, D and others (2001) Extent of regretted sexual intercourse among young teenagers in Scotland: a cross sectional study. *British Medical Journal,* 320, 243–4

UNICEF (2001) A league table of teenage births in rich nations, *Innocenti Report Card,* 3. Florence: UNICEF Innocenti Research Centre.

JOIN NCB

national
children's
bureau
making a difference

Join NCB to ensure that you are not missing out on our extensive range of resources which cover a host of issues affecting schools, including:

- race equality
- SEN codes of practice
- pupil inclusion strategies
- PSHE and citizenship
- peer support
- anti-bullying
- drug, sex and health education.

NCB produces a wide range of books, newsletters and factsheets.

NCB offers training for teachers and others involved in schools. We run courses which reflect current trends and new legislation. We can develop and deliver 'tailor-made' courses, based on our work and adapted to the needs of individual schools.

Recent training courses have covered sex and relationships education, race equality in schools, mentoring, peer support, SENDA and accessibility strategies. We also offer courses on PSHE and Citizenship.

Further information:

For information about membership call 020 7843 6080, e-mail membership@ncb.org.uk or visit www.ncb.org.uk/membership

For information about publications visit www.ncb.org.uk/publications

For further information about training opportunities and to discuss your needs call 020 7843 1906, e-mail training@ncb.org.uk or visit www.ncb.org.uk/events

National Children's Bureau, registered charity no. 258825. 8 Wakley Street, London EC1V 7QE